Hippopotamuses

For Kids

Amazing Animal Books

for Young Readers

By Zahra Jazeel and John Davidson

Mendon Cottage Books

Mendon Cottage Books

JD-Biz Corp Publishing

Read More Amazing Animal Books

Purchase at Amazon.com

Table of Contents

Introduction

Which animal comes to your mind when you hear the word 'Africa'? Lion, elephant, hyena? If you did think of those animals, you're surely missing on something big. Let me give you a clue. Seeing this animal for the first time, one may think it is fat and clumsy. But no, it's not the rhino we're talking about. It's the hippopotamus!

Join us as we try to explore the world of hippos like you've never known before. We provide you with an insight into the life of a hippo describing every aspect of them from characteristics to feeding habits, behaviors, communication methods and many species both living and extinct. What's more? We have even got you a summary of some fun facts about hippos that would raise your eyebrows for sure!

About Hippopotamuses

Hippopotamus, simply called as hippo is derived from the Greek term 'river horse'. Why is the hippo called a 'river horse'? The answer lies in the question itself. Hippopotamuses simply love water, even though they are semiaquatic which means they live partly on water and partly on land. They inhabit mostly on lakes, rivers and mangrove swamps. Hippos have a barrel shaped body with enormous mouth and teeth. Their legs look short and stubby with skin being almost entirely hairless. Hippos are large and prefer to eat plant matter mostly. Living in sub-Saharan Africa, these mammals secure the 3rd place for being the largest type of land mammals just after the elephant and the rhinoceros. Not only that, they are deemed to be one of the largest quadrupeds too. A quadruped is an animal having four feet.

Though a hippopotamus resemble a pig physically, it may be surprising to learn that their closest living relatives are cetaceans. Cetaceans are marine mammals which commonly include whales, porpoises and dolphins. They parted from hippos 55 million years ago. Hippopotamuses are the heaviest extant artiodactyl! That means they are the heaviest existing animal with an even number of toes. Despite their clumsy look and short legs, they can outrun a human easily as they can reach a speed of up to 30km/hr over short distances. Now you don't want to mess with these creatures to risk a bite from their canines. Do you?

Preserved remains of an animal, plant or other organisms from the past are called fossils. They are important sources of data to analyze many things about a long lost animal or a plant, not to mention small microscopic organisms. The earliest fossils of a hippopotamus from Africa date back to about 15 million years.

Hippos look cute and harmless. But do not be fooled by their appearance. They are ranked among Africa's most dangerous animals. There is a good reason behind it. Hippopotamuses are aggressive and have an unpredictable behavior. But they remain threatened due to habitat destruction and poaching for their flesh and ivory teeth. Now that does sound a lot like an African rhino's fate.

Hippopotamuses stay cool during daytime by wallowing in water or mud. Their skin has to be kept wet in order to prevent dehydration. Hence they spend about 16 hours a day in water. After the sun had set, they emerge from water to graze on grasses overland. They may even travel a distance of 10km on a single night which could take 6 hours. Grazing takes place solitarily. Unlike in water, they are not territorial on land. A hippo calf weighs around 45kg at birth. Every 2 years, females have only one calf. Immediately after birth, mother and the baby hippo join the rest of the hippos for protection from predators such as lions, crocodiles and hyenas. When hippos feel threatened on land, they run towards water. On average, they consume about 35-40kg a night. But this is less when compared to their body weight. The largest cattle consume 2.5% of their body weight every day. But a hippopotamus consumes only 1-1.5% of their body weight in comparison.

Characteristics

If you look closely at a hippopotamus you will be able to notice that despite their plump, bulky body and stumpy legs, their weight is evenly distributed among their feet and within toes to support them on land. Their toes are webbed which allows them to move about in water as well as shallow river bottoms quite easily. You may think that their short legs are a disadvantage to them. But no. Their legs help in providing strong propulsions when moving through water. Propulsion is a force that helps to move something forward. The positioning of their eyes, ears and nostrils above their head helps them to stay submerged in water while still being able to see, hear and breathe. Hippopotamuses have a slate or a purple grey colored skin. Pinkish brown coloration could be seen around their ears and eyes. Hair- like bristles are present on their tails and heads.

A hippopotamus's skin is 15cm thick. This acts as a protective cover against predators or conspecifies, meaning organisms of the same species. In this case, they are other hippos. Usually, a hippopotamus weighs between 1300 to 3200kg. A male hippo can be easily identified from a female hippo as the former appears to be 200kg larger than the latter at maturity and can put on several kg with age. This could be possible because the males continue to grow throughout their life unlike females who at the age of 25 would reach their maximum weight. Muzzles of the males are larger and they possess a greater jaw area than the females apart from their size. Generally, females reach a length of about 345cm. But a male's maximum length could be around 505cm. One of the most distinctive features of a hippo is their tusks. These tasks are not like an elephant's tusks. Tusks of a hippopotamus refer to their two long, sharp canine teeth present in their lower jaw. Did you know that the largest hippo ever to be recorded was a male weighing 4,500kg which was held captive in Munich, Germany?

The jaw of a hippopotamus can open wide up to 150 degrees to display their sharp, enormous incisors and canines. Incisors grow up to 40cm while canines grow up to 50cm. When grazing, hippos sharpen themselves while grinding. Though they seem well adapted for a life in water, they cannot stay afloat, let alone swim! Their bodies are too dense for that. They simply bounce and walk along the river beds by touching the bottom lightly with their toes.

How can a hippo stay submerged without water entering them? We have the answer to that. They fold their ears and close their nostrils. This allows them to hold their breath and stay underwater for about 5 minutes or more. Did you know that a hippo can sleep underwater? Just like we blink when a ball is thrown at our face, there is a reflex mechanism in a hippo to enable them this activity. This allows them to pop up, then take a breath and sink down while still asleep. Amazing huh?

Hippos do not have sweat or scent glands. Instead, they secrete a red oily substance from their skin which many people used to call as 'Blood sweat'. This fluid is actually made of 2 pigments namely hipposudoric acid which is red, and norhippossudoric acid which is orange. Both are highly acidic and act as a sunscreen while preventing the growth of bacteria which cause diseases. Initially, the secretion is colorless but turns orange-red when exposed to sun. The average lifespan of a hippopotamus ranges between 40-50 years.

Distribution

Hippopotamuses are found living throughout the rivers of savannah in Africa and along the main rivers in Central Africa. Though they are exclusively found in the Ethiopian region, known populations exist in countries such as Liberia, Angola, Gambia, Nigeria, Ethiopia, Burundi, Cameroon, Rwanda, Somalia, Sudan, Uganda, Zimbabwe, Tanzania, Kenya, Namibia, Malawi, Central African republic, republic of Congo, Ghana, sierra Leone, Swaziland, Zambia, Guinea, Togo and South Africa. They were thought to be widespread in Europe and North Africa during the late Pleistocene and Eemian eva, 2 of the significant periods in the earth's history about 30,000 years back. Hippopotamus was a common species occupying near the Egypt's Nile region until it was totally removed.

Hippos live in both forest and savannah areas. In the mid-1970s, the population of hippopotamuses in the Virunga National park of democratic republic of Congo dropped from 29,000 to 800 or 900. This was a dramatic decline caused by the disruptions during the 2nd Congo war. Poachers were thought to be poorly paid soldiers of

Congo known as the Mai – Mai rebels. Hippos were poached for financial gain and the belief of hippos being harmful to the society. Though the selling of meat is illegal, officers from Virunga National Park are unable to track the sales in black markets.

There are no recorded data about the specific size of a hippopotamus's territory. But the size mainly depends on the availability of food, water and the number of individuals in a herd.

Diet

Hippopotamuses follow their familiar paths known as the 'hippo paths' in search of grassy areas around waterbeds after dusk. They prefer feeding on short grass patches known as 'hippo lawns' which are situated close to water. But when food becomes scare, they are known to travel several miles in search of food looking for new rivers or lakes. Their keen sense of hearing will aid them to hear the sounds of fruits falling and their good sense of smell will help them sniff out any tasty treats to consume. Since hippos lead a sedentary lifestyle which means a life which does not require much physical activity, much of their energy is conserved.

When grazing, the hippos graze in circular patterns of 3-4km. Their diet mainly consists of grasses, small shoots and reeds. Though they do not dig for fruits or roots, they will consume different types of plants when they are available. Their lips which are muscular and wide are built to pull up grasses. Unlike other type of herbivores, hippopotamuses do not chew their food. In order to conserve the nutrition value, they tear and soften the grasses. Hippos return to their grazing spot before dawn entering their water pools at the same spot where they left. In rare instances, they are found to rest in nearby pools before returning the following nightfall. This occurs if the hippo had a long trip. Though a hippo's stomach is not meant for digesting meat, they sometimes feed on dead animals close to their pools. This behavior occurs due to nutritional deficiencies or illness.

Behavior

Hippopotamuses are very social creatures and they live in groups containing about 20 to 100 members. Since they lead an inactive lifestyle, most of their day is spent on resting. Many of their activities take place at night. Usually the males rule in different animal hierarchies. But in hippos, this is different as the females act as the leaders in a herd having control of the resting pools. Generally, the males rest on the outskirts of pools in order to protect the females and calves. Males tend to compete for dominance at the age of 7. This behavior is exhibited through roaring, jaw clashing, yawning and dung showering. Dominant males do not tolerate young males who attempt to challenge them. Hence there is likelihood for them to kill the young ones during these clashes. Territorial behaviors are exhibited through honking, wheezing and dung showing.

When engaging in dung showering, a hippo lifts its rear and scatters the excreta with its tail into the unfamiliar territory. They also spread their dung along their grazing paths as well as the shoreline. During dry season when the resources get scarce and the population gets crowded, intense fights break out. Defensive behaviors such as biting, yawning and tusk clashing takes place when males fight to protect the herd from predators.

Basically, the diet of a hippo consists entirely of grass with a minimum portion of it being aquatic plants. There are reported rare cases of cannibalism seen among hippos. This means they have eaten the flesh of hippos on rare instances. But this behavior is believed to be of sick hippos and considered an unhealthy behavior. In water, adult hippos move to a rate of 5 mph resurfacing at every 3-5 minute interval in order to breathe. A baby hippo requires 2-3 minute intervals. Some species of fish helps clean the mouth of a hippo by picking on all the food stuck in between its teeth. Here, the hippo gets cleaned and the fish gets the food. Both parties are happy at the end of the day.

Hippopotamuses are very aggressive. They fight to protect their territories against intruders or predators . Crocodiles are their usual rivals. When fights break out, crocodiles are either driven out or killed by the hippos.

Communication and Perception

Hippopotamuses are highly social animals. Hence they also communicate with each other just like us humans. Their commination methods are much different than ours though. In order to communicate, they use a wide range of surface and under water sounds. Since they are very much adapted to aquatic lifestyle, such sounds are considered a necessity. The honking call which is made by exhaled breath is the most common form of communication used by submerged hippos. This is made to alert the others about possible threats. This call can be so loud as a thunder and turn into a chorus if the other males join in.

One special ability the hippopotamuses possess is their capability to communicate both above and below the water at the same instance. Sounds made above the surface come through the nostrils but they are made in the voice box called the larynx just under water. These signals are important to express information regarding territorial boundaries or the location of other hippos. Other than these, visual displays such as yawning, wheezing, honking and dung showering take place during territorial clashes.

Ecosystem Roles

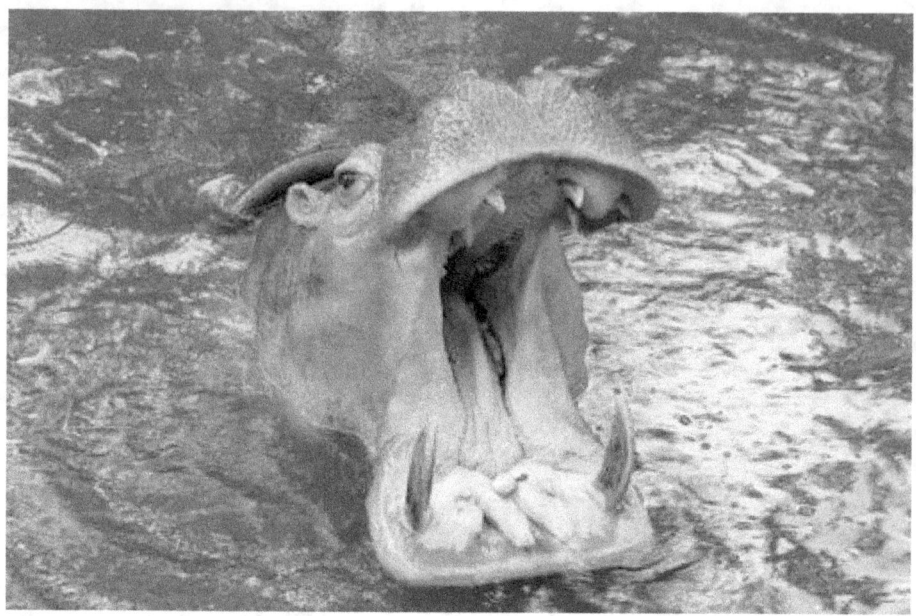

Hippopotamuses play a major role in the ecosystem due to their enormous size. They help in creating habitats for small organisms. The hippo path that they create from water to land when searching for food enables to clear avenues for the water to flow during wet seasons. Lagoons and side pools are created when flooding takes place on these paths which allows small fish to swim to these areas when droughts occur.

Several parasitic forms are present both inside and outside of a hippo's body. Parasites that are found living outside a hippo's body are called ectoparasites. The presence of ticks and leeches around their anal region is no surprise as they have an aquatic lifestyle. There are no damages or serious injuries due to these parasites other than irritation and blood loss. Young hippopotamuses carry liver flukes which is also a type of parasite in their liver. This gives the idea that hippos build up resistance against the parasite with age.

Humans and Hippos

The interaction between humans and hippos existed around 160,000 years back as suggested by some early evidence. Engravings and rock paintings indicating humans having hunted hippos are found in the mountains of Central Sahara dating back to 4,000 or 5,000 years. The Romans and Greeks knew about hippopotamus. Herodotus, a Greek historian had described about hippopotamus in his work of arts. Even lions do not match the courage of a hippopotamus. That is why the Zulu warriors prefer to be brave like a hippopotamus.

Hippopotamuses are popular as zoo animals. The 1st hippo to arrive at a zoo attracted around 10,000 visitors each day. This took place in

May 25th 1850 at the London Zoo. Since hippos are expensive to maintain, many claim that this could be the reason for their low birth rates in captivity than in wild. Hippos are known to attack humans on boats or land with no real provocation. This shows their aggressiveness towards humans.

Hippopotamuses are depicted in different cultures and folklore. They are featured especially in African folktales. The hippopotamuses have also found their way towards television shows and cartoons. It is interesting to note that their character is used to create humor in Disney films like 'Fantasia' and 'Madagascar'.

Extinct Species

Malagasy hippopotamus, also known as the Malagasy pygmy hippopotamus and Malagasy dwarf hippopotamus which lived in Madagascar is an extinct species of hippopotamus. There were 3 other species of hippos from the above species which is thought to have become extinct during the Holocene era, one of them strongly believed to have lived at least 1000 years before. The Malagasy hippopotamuses were small in size when compared to the modern hippopotamuses. This could be due to a process called insular dwarfism. Insular dwarfism is a condition where reductions of sizes occur in large animals through generations due to their population's range being limited to small environments such as an island.

Evidences from fossil records suggest that many Malagasy hippos were hunted by humans which could have been the possible reason for their gradual extinction. However, isolated Malagasy hippos could have survived in remote areas as some villages claimed of seeing such animals in 1976 though researchers were unable to find evidence for that being true.

There were 2 other species of hippos known as the H.gorgops and European hippopotamus. They ranged across Europe and the British isles. But they both are believed to have become extinct before the period of last glaciation. Glaciation is a process of glacier formation. Both the above species were bigger than the modern ones that we know today. However it is believed that the ancestors of the European hippos moved to the Mediterranean islands during the Pleistocene era. Many dwarf species survived in this era. But the debate on whether humans were behind all these extinctions continues even till today while some others claim that the focus right now should be to protect the hippos present today.

Common Hippopotamus

The common hippopotamus weighs approximately 3 tons. Out of the 2 remaining species of hippos, they're the largest. Ancient Egyptians considered hippos to be a symbol of fertility and strength. A hippo's protective nature towards their young is one fact that they valued a lot. Common hippopotamuses are found living across East African tropical areas in water bodies such as rivers, lakes and swamps. Although they prefer water that is not deep and possess a soft bottom, they also like clean water that does not move very much. When the African sun gets really hot, these areas are where they will turn to in order to keep cool.

Having a huge appetite had been a loss to the local farmers as common hippopotamus are well reputed for destroying large amount of crops these farmers cultivate for their own survival. Common hippos live groups. Each group may be very small or large depending on the number of individuals. They are highly territorial in water. There is a lot of aggression among males in a herd as they fight for space and mating rights. The males and females keep away from each other as far as they can. Female hippos with their cubs form sub groups and look after the young hippos of each other whenever possible.

Common hippopotamuses have only a few predators. The reason is that many other animals fear them. However when food becomes scarce, animals such as alligators, hyenas and crocodiles try to bring down a young common hippo though it requires patience to even find one out of its mother's reach. The common hippopotamus's biggest enemies are humans. Consuming hippo meat is a common practice of African villagers.

Pygmy Hippopotamus

Pygmy hippopotamuses are smaller than common hippopotamuses. Many people find the whole body of this hippo quite impressive. The middle section is their biggest portion of their body while their legs remain short and stocky. They have a tiny tail that looks really out of place. In contrary, their head and mouth looks large with teeth made of ivory. This is the common cause for which they are hunted. They have a very keen sense of hearing and their vision is well adapted for both day and night. Since they are active at night, they spend their day time lazing around in water.

Pygmy hippos are very powerful and protective of their territory. Conflicts in water are a common occurrence. If you look at a herd, you will be able to see the different social groups existing in that area. Females with their young ones are together in a group while females without young form another group. Bachelor males are together in a group whereas the dominant bull stays alone. Hippos are among the noisiest in Africa. It could be quite fascinating to listen to all their commotions. Pygmy hippos in general are very vocal.

The skin of a pygmy hippo is similar to a common hippo. Baby pygmy hippos weigh around 60 pounds at birth. Many predators see them as a source of food. But still, they often keep away as they know that an angry encounter from a mother hippo can put them to rest forever.

Fun facts about hippos

The hippopotamus is close to the size of a white rhinoceros.

Their stomach is like a storage sack. It can store grass worth of 2 days and go on without eating for three weeks.

For how many minutes can you hold your breath under water? I bet for some, it may be less than a minute. But an adult hippo is capable of holding its breath for 30 minutes.

In the rivers of Africa, hippopotamuses look very much like floating islands as the birds try to fish while perched firmly on their backs. Sometimes even baby crocodiles as well as turtles are seen basking on hippos.

A group of fish is called a school and a group of birds is called a flock. But what do you call a group of hippos? A group of hippos is called a pod, bloat or siege.

Several species of fish in Africa benefit from the dead skin cells and the food remnants of a hippo.

Male, female and baby hippopotamuses are called by different names. A female hippo is called a cow whereas a male hippo is called a bull. The baby hippo is addressed as a calf.

How much can a hippo hide weigh? It can weigh about half a ton!

Author Bio

Fathima Zahra Jazeel

Was born in Sri Lanka and completed her G.C.E Advanced Level in the Bio Science stream. She completed her BTEC Level IV Edexcel Professional Diploma in Teaching in the year 2013 and currently works as a teacher while following the BTEC Level V Edexcel Professional Diploma in Advanced Teaching leading to a professional degree. Her passion for journalism made her engage in writing for both local as well as international newsmagazines.

Her family had been rearing parrots as pets for decades which motivated her to be a local voluntary social worker to create awareness about conserving animals in the wild.

Our books are available at

1. Amazon.com

2. Barnes and Noble

3. Itunes

4. Kobo

5. Smashwords

6. Google Play Books

This book is published by

JD-Biz Corp

P O Box 374

Mendon, Utah 84325

http://www.jd-biz.com/

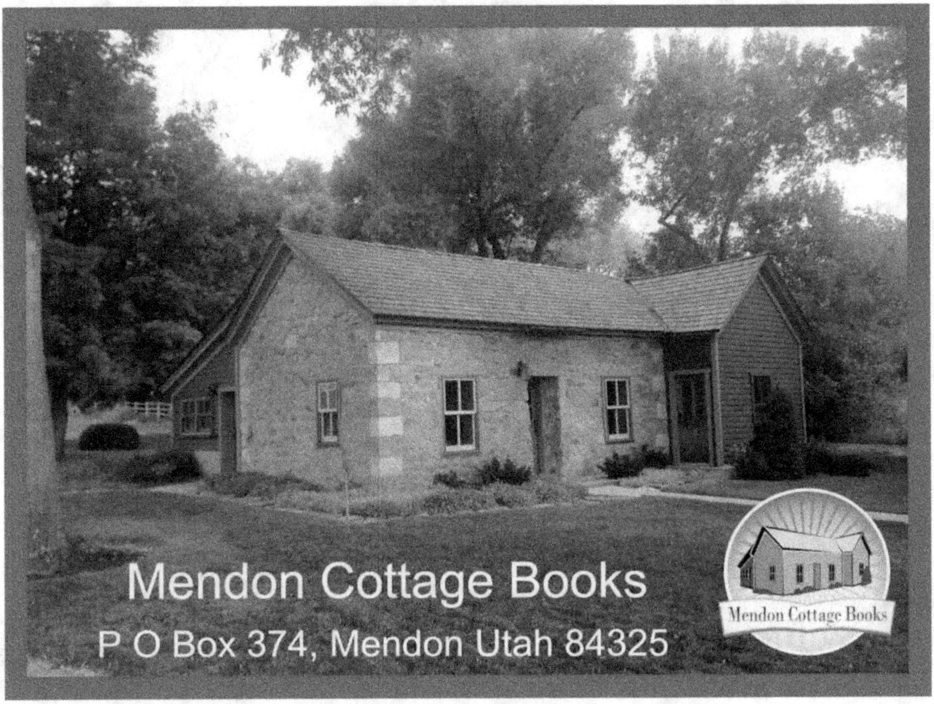

Mendon Cottage Books

P O Box 374, Mendon Utah 84325

Mendon Cottage Books

Top Ten Dog Breeds For Kids

Amazing Animal Books
For Young Readers
Kisha Bennett & John Davidson

Poodles

Dog Books for Kids
K. Bennett

Labrador Retrievers

Dog Books for Kids
K. Bennett

German Shepherds

Dog Books for Kids
K. Bennett

Rottweilers

Dog Books for Kids
K. Bennett

Boxers

Dog Books for Kids
K. Bennett

Golden Retrievers

Dog Books for Kids
K. Bennett

Beagles

Dog Books for Kids
K. Bennett

Yorkies

Dog Books for Kids
K. Bennett

Horses
For Kids
Amazing Animal Books
For Young Readers
By John and
Annalee Davidson

Wolves
For Kids
Amazing Animal Books
For Young Readers
By John Davidson and Virginia Fidler

Lady Bugs
For Kids
Amazing Animal Books
For Young Readers
By Jean Hall & John Davidson

Sasquatch - Yeti
Abominable Snowman
Bigfoot
Amazing Animal Books
For Young Readers
By John Davidson

Penguins
For Kids
Amazing Animal Books
For Young Readers
Kim Chase & John Davidson

Komodo Dragons
For Kids

Amazing Animal Books
For Young Readers
By Lisa Barry & John Davidson

Cats
For Kids

Amazing Animal Books
For Young Readers
K. Bennett & John Davidson

Spiders

For Kids
Amazing Animal Books
For Young Readers
By John Davidson

Giant Panda Bears
For Kids
Amazing Animal Books
For Young Readers
By John Davidson

Animals of North America

For Kids
Amazing Animal Books
For Young Readers
By John Davidson

Birds of North America
For Kids

Amazing Animal Books
For Young Readers
By John Davidson

Dolphins
For Kids

Amazing Animal Books
For Young Readers
By John Davidson and Natalia Asfar

Hamsters

For Kids
Amazing Animal Books
For Young Readers
John Davidson

Polar Bears

For Kids
Amazing Animal Books
For Young Readers
By John Davidson and Kim Chase

Turtles
For Kids

Amazing Animal Books
For Young Readers
By John Davidson and Natalia Asfar

Walruses
For Kids

Amazing Animal Books
For Young Readers
By John Davidson and Kim Chase

My First Book About
Animals of Australia

Amazing Animal Books
By Annalee and John Davidson
Children's Picture Books

Goats
For Kids

Amazing Animal Books
For Young Readers
Rachel Smith & John Davidson

Flamingos
For Kids

Amazing Animal Books
For Young Readers
K. Bennett & John Davidson

Giraffes
For Kids

Amazing Animal Books
For Young Readers
Valeria Arcas & John Davidson

Eagles

For Kids
Amazing Animal Books
For Young Readers
Nicholas Williams & John Davidson

Bears
For Kids
Amazing Animal Books
For Young Readers
Zahra Jazeel & John Davidson

Parrots
For Kids

Amazing Animal Books
For Young Readers
Zahra Jazeel & John Davidson

My First Book About
Kittens

Amazing Animal Books
By John Davidson
Children's Picture Books

Sharks

For Kids
Amazing Animal Books
For Young Readers
By John Davidson

Monkeys

Amazing Animal Books
For Young Readers
By John and
Annalee Davidson

Whales
Amazing Animal Books
For Young Readers
By John Davidson

Kittens
Amazing Animal Books
For Young Readers
By John Davidson

Meerkats
For Kids
Amazing Animal Books
For Young Readers
John Davidson and Lisa Barry

Elephants
For Kids

Amazing Animal Books
For Young Readers
Kim Chase & John Davidson

Big Mammals of Yellowstone
For Kids

Amazing Animal Books
For Young Readers
By John Davidson

Big Cats
For Kids
Amazing Animal Books
For Young Readers
By John Davidson

My First Book About Pandas

Amazing Animal Books
By Annalee and John Davidson
BEST
Children's Picture Books

Chinchillas

For Kids
Amazing Animal Books
For Young Readers
John Davidson and Jaime Whymburger

Beavers
For Kids

Amazing Animal Books
For Young Readers
By J Davidson

Bees

Amazing Animal Books
For Young Readers
By J Davidson and Jennifer Lejeune

Animals of Australia
For Kids
Amazing Animal Books
For Young Readers
By John Davidson
and Shawn Vincent Wilson

Frogs
For Kids
Amazing Animal Books
For Young Readers
By John Davidson

My First Book About Frogs
Amazing Animal Books
By John Davidson
Children's Picture Books

Tigers

For Kids
Amazing Animal Books
For Young Readers
Kim Chase & John Davidson

Scorpions
For Kids

Amazing Animal Books
For Young Readers
John Davidson

Snakes

For Kids
Amazing Animal Books
For Young Readers
By John Davidson and Nadine Theis

Animals of Africa
For Kids

Amazing Animal Books
For Young Readers
Steve Mufun & John Davidson

Dinosaurs

For Kids
Amazing Animal Books
For Young Readers
By John Davidson

Sharks
For Kids

Amazing Animal Books
For Young Readers
By John Davidson

Spiders
For Kids

Amazing Animal Books
For Young Readers
By John Davidson

Giant Panda Bears

Amazing Animal Books
For Young Readers
By John Davidson

Giraffes
For Kids

Amazing Animal Books
For Young Readers
Valeria Arcas & John Davidson

Eagles

For Kids
Amazing Animal Books
For Young Readers
Nicholas Williams & John Davidson

Bears
For Kids
Amazing Animal Books
For Young Readers
Zahra Jazeel & John Davidson

www.ingramcontent.com/pod-product-compliance
Lightning Source LLC
Chambersburg PA
CBHW061943280526
45787CB00004B/1711